T0346402

Good food
after weight loss surgery

Professor Kristel De Vogelaere

Good food
after weight loss surgery

Recipes by a surgeon
for patients, family and friends

Photography by Thierry Van Vreckem

LANNOO

Contents

Foreword

If you are a specialist in weight loss surgery, it goes without saying that you are confronted day after day with hundreds of different questions, not only about the surgery itself, but also about the life that can be led and the food that can be eaten once the surgery has been performed.

In my free time, I love to cook. Cooking makes me happy. With this cook book I hope that I can also help to make my patients happy, by showing them that you can still eat delicious food after weight loss surgery.

This book has been written especially for those patients, but also for their families and friends, who wonder what they should make for their meals together, as well as for anyone who is contemplating weight loss surgery.

Because so many half truths are told by the media (with the internet leading the way), I thought that it was important to provide some general guidance about recommended eating habits after a weight loss operation.

The colorful and tasty recipes in this book show that your diet after the operation does not need to be boring and bland. On the contrary, I hope that these recipes will act as a source of inspiration for you to eat healthily and enjoyably with your family and friends for the rest of your days.

Professor Kristel De Vogelaere

Prof.Dr De Vogelaere Kristel
Abdominaal Chirurg
RIZIV : 1-08471-72-140

MONT
BLANC
60 ml INK

BLUE

Prof.Dr. DE VOGELAERE Kristel
Chirurg
1-08471-72-140

Introduction

Choosing to undergo weight loss surgery is probably one of the most difficult decisions that anyone has to make. This surgery is different from any other kind of surgery. Most surgery involves a clear recovery period, after which the patient is 'cured'. End of story. But with weight loss surgery the real work, both physical and emotional, only begins after the operation has been performed – and it continues your whole life long. The operation itself is just a first small step on a long road to success. What happens afterwards is entirely in your own hands.

Many aspects of your life will change. Old and destructive habits will need to make way for new challenges. You will notice many changes in the way you live – but they will be changes for the better. However, it will not be easy: new eating habits, a healthier lifestyle, different clothes... It is necessary to make time for these changes – and for yourself. It is also important to find support among your family, friends and other people who have undergone the same surgery.

It is equally important to have a good guide, a handbook to show you the road you need to follow in your new life. This book focuses on just one aspect of that new life: food. And not just food, but good food. Good food

that is ideal for people who have had weight loss surgery, thanks to the specially adapted recipes. Good food that also takes account of family and friends who want to support 'their' patient. All the dishes are suitable for non-patients who want to eat better and more healthily. Each recipe is designed to serve four people. The patient will eat a maximum of one cup or 100-200 grams as their portion, or less if satiation – the feeling of fullness – is reached more quickly (especially in the early stages).

The additional tips and eating guidelines (given later on in this introduction) will make it possible for you to maximize your weight loss.

I hope that my book will make life easier for you after your operation and will help you to find your way with a minimum of difficulty through the various post-operative phases.

Although the decision to undergo weight loss surgery was doubtless not an easy one, time will show that it was nevertheless the best option – providing you follow the strictly defined rules. After years of fighting against those excess kilos, you will once again be able to enjoy a more active, more comfortable, more socially enriching and healthier life.

Eating after weight loss surgery

Portions

A normal stomach has a large intake capacity and can stretch in size when necessary. After weight loss surgery the capacity of the stomach is significantly reduced. This means that patients need to eat smaller portions. It is recommended to eat six small portions per day, in part because the passage of food between the esophagus and the stomach is sometimes more difficult than before (especially with a gastric band).

Satiety or feeling full

It is of great importance to be able to recognize the moment when you are satiated or feel full. Once you have had enough and 'can eat no more', you must stop eating, even if your portion is not fully consumed. If you continue eating, the result will be an uncomfortable or even painful sensation, with nausea and vomiting. In the initial phase, the 'new' stomach can be 'full' after as little as two tablespoons. After a number of weeks, the new stomach's capacity will gradually increase, so that you can eat a whole cup.

Building up new eating habits

Building up a new pattern of eating habits after weight loss surgery is not something that happens from one day to the next. There are different phases: a fluid or semi-fluid phase; a pureed phase; a light food phase; and finally a phase with normal, balanced eating.

Phase 1: liquid food

During this first phase (2-4 weeks), it is recommended that you should only eat liquid or semi-liquid foods, such as pap, pastes, custard and yoghurt without sugar (but with a sweetener, if necessary). For the first few days it is often difficult to drink the quantities of fluids that are recommended. Taking small sips and drinking slowly will help. A whole chapter later in the book is devoted to soups, which are easy to ingest in this initial phase. Smoothies are another good alternative to 'normal' food. Fruit juices and a thin broth are also acceptable.

Phase 2: semi-soft food

It will gradually become possible to switch to mixed or pureed food. It is important that these dishes do not contain any solid pieces. It is for this reason that later in the book you will find recipes for vegetable purees, which you can eat with ground meat or fish. In this second phase, which also lasts 2-4 weeks, it is advisable to blend all your food in a mixer, so that it is easier to eat.

Phase 3: light food

The following transition is to light food; in other words, soft and tender foods, such as ground or very finely diced meat and boiled vegetables. These foods should be eaten in six small portions spread throughout the day. You need to persist with this phase for at least four weeks, before finally moving on to normal food.

Phase 4: normal food

You can now eat carefully chosen, well balanced selections of normal 'solid' food, which you must chew thoroughly before swallowing. Slow eating is still the message.

The right choices

Because the amount of food you eat is very small, it is important to choose products that contain plenty of protein, but with the fewest calories. Proteins are vital for the recovery of your body after the operation. The digestion of some foodstuffs, particularly with hard fibers (raw vegetables, unripe fresh fruit, etc.), will be slower and/or more difficult.

Fruit

A good alternative to fruit is unsweetened fruit juice. However, you should drink these in moderation, because the higher concentration of fruit sugar means that juices of this kind are calorie-rich. Other options include fruit puree without sugar (but with a sweetener) or conserved fruits in their own juices (peaches, apricots), cut into small pieces and well chewed before swallowing. The fibers and skins in citrus fruits can sometimes cause problems, because they are hard to digest and may lead to vomiting.

Vegetables

The skins and seeds of vegetables (for example, tomatoes and bell peppers) are best avoided, because they are difficult to digest. For this reason, all the vegetables in our recipes are peeled and de-seeded. Start with mixed vegetables or a vegetable puree and switch gradually to stewed or boiled vegetables. Avoid high-fiber vegetables, such as asparagus, celery and legumes, because you will have a lower tolerance for them.

Meat

Choose lean types of meat. You will find ground meat and other minced preparations easier to digest. Meat that is too dry, too tough or contains too many long fibers, such as stewing steak and beefsteak, is inclined to 'lodge' in your stomach, with all the unpleasant consequences this entails. It is therefore important to avoid eating your meat 'dry'. Use a little light meat sauce, fish sauce, vegetable sauce, stock or skimmed milk.

Fish

Fish does not have a fibrous structure and is easy to eat. For preference, choose oily types of fish (like salmon or mackerel), because of their high levels of omega-3 fatty acids. Our bodies need these essential nutrients to function properly. Research has shown that omega-3 fatty acids can help to prevent heart and vascular disease.

Fats and oils

Use a minimum of greasing and cooking fats. Choose fats that are high in unsaturated and low in saturated fat content. In our recipes, we always use olive oil.

Carbohydrates

Fresh bread, fresh sandwiches and the white crusts of baguettes and bread rolls will be difficult for you to digest. They form little 'dough balls' in your stomach, which are unable to pass through the opening. Toasted sandwiches, crackers, rusks and other crisp breads are a good alternative.

Drink

Avoid gaseous/carbonated drinks (or first remove the gas by stirring with a spoon). Drinking too much of these effervescent drinks can give you a bloated feeling and wind. Drink sufficient fluids (at least 1.5 liters per day), but never eat and drink at the same time. Leave (before and afterwards!) at least half an hour between eating and drinking. Avoid sugared drinks, because of their high calorie content. Moderate your intake of alcoholic drinks. Light vegetable soups, stocks, water, tea and coffee should provide sufficient variation.

Cheese and dairy products

Eat sufficient dairy products, because they are a good source of calcium and vitamin B12. In general, cheeses should not cause you any problems and there are plenty of different types: quark, spread cheese, cottage cheese, soft cheese, etc. Use cheeses with a low fat content.

Tips

- Avoid foods with a high fat or sugar content.
- Use sweeteners (such as stevia) instead of sugar.
- Use skimmed or semi-skimmed milk. If required, use light cream in your recipes. In many of the recipes in this book I give a preference for sour cream, yoghurt, low-fat cottage cheese or cream cheese.

Physical exercise

Overweight people probably took very little physical exercise before their weight loss surgery. This is something that needs to change after the operation! Fortunately, after a time this will cease to be a 'chore', and will instead become a pleasure, since you will find physical activities easier and more rewarding. It will also help you to maintain your reduced weight. Healthy exercise helps to optimize the positive results of the operation and limits muscle deterioration during the weight reduction phase.

What should you be trying to achieve? Half an hour a day is enough. That's all it takes! And I am not talking about 'serious', inten-sive sport: swimming, cycling, walking or light fitness exercises are all fine. It is easy to build physical exercise into your day-to-day routine: take the bike instead of the car; do your daily shopping on foot; take the stairs instead of the lift; park your car some distance from where you want to go, so that you need to walk the rest of the way. Using a step counter will give you some idea of how much exercise you are taking each day, so that you can gradually increase the amount.

You should start your program of physical exercise from the second week after the operation. Begin with some light walking or swimming. After six weeks, you can in-crease the intensity of your training.

Lifelong guidelines

- Eat small quantities (maximum 100-200 grams per meal, six times a day).
- Do not miss out any meals.
- Eat and drink slowly.
- Eat regularly.
- Take sufficient time to eat (20-30 minutes). Eating too fast causes nausea and vomiting.
- Do not talk while you are eating.
- Take small mouthfuls and chew them until they are mush before you swallow; otherwise, pieces of food may become lodged uncomfortably in your digestive system.
- Only take the next mouthful when you have swallowed the preceding one.
- Drink between meals and not during meals (1.5 liters per day).
- Stop eating and drinking as soon as you feel full. Eating more will cause you to vomit.
- Make a varied choice of food based on the food triangle. Don't just always pick the things you like the most; pick things that are good for you as well.
- Try new foods on a regular basis.
- You may sometimes experience constipation. Fresh fruit juice and sufficient fibers should help to combat this problem.
- Avoid carbonated drinks and alcohol.
- Avoid excessive use of sugar, sweets and fats (replace saturated with unsaturated fats in your diet).
- Take vitamin and mineral supplements.
- Take half an hour of exercise each day.

Weight loss surgery

Using surgery as a means to lose weight is never a first-choice option. People with overweight or *obestitas* (obesity) usually only take this step after numerous failed attempts to shed their excess kilos via various diets, exercise programs, medication, etc. Surgery is an acceptable approach in certain circumstances and under certain conditions: you must be at least 18 years of age; you must have been following (unsuccessfully) at least one year of weight loss treatment under the guidance of a dietician; you must have a body mass index (BMI) of 40 or more (35 or more if you also suffer from diabetes, untreatable high blood pressure or sleep apnoea, or have already undergone unsuccessful weight loss surgery).

The BMI is a much more accurate way to determine whether or not someone is overweight than simply weighing them. To calculate your BMI you divide your body weight in kilograms by the square of your height. Imagine that you weigh 120 kilos and are 1.60 meters tall: your body mass is therefore 120 / 2.56 (1.60 x 1.60) = 46.9.

According to the World Health Organization, a BMI of more than 40 is defined as 'morbidly obese', a situation that can involve serious health risks for the person concerned. A BMI of more than 30 is defined as 'obese'. More than 25 is 'overweight'. A healthy BMI is between 18.5 and 25. In recent times, more use has also been made of the measuring of the abdominal circumference as a reference factor for overweight.

There are two different kinds of weight loss surgery: *restrictive surgery* reduces the size of the stomach; *malabsorptive surgery* reduces calorie intake through the small intestine by 'shortcutting' sections of that intestine. Most of the operations are carried out using the 'keyhole' technique, otherwise known as a laparoscopy.

The most well-known and also the most common type of malabsorptive surgery is the bypass. With this operation no part of the stomach is physically removed. Instead, a small pouch is made that serves as a new and smaller stomach. The food consumed by the patient is 'diverted' into this pouch, to which a loop of intestine is attached. This loop transfers the food in an undigested state. As a result, the body's digestive juices only come into contact with the food at a much later stage in the digestive process, so that fewer calories can be absorbed – but also fewer nutrients, such as iron, calcium and vitamins.

With restrictive surgery, the manner in which calories and nutrients are absorbed remains essentially unaltered, but patients eat less because their reduced stomach is more quickly full. The most common restrictive techniques are the gastric band and the sleeve gastrectomy (the stomach reduction operation).

A gastric band is positioned around the entrance to the stomach, so that a kind of forestomach is created. The smaller size of this forestomach means that the patient feels full more quickly and therefore eats less. The gastric band is a reversible technique and is particularly suitable for people who simply eat too much. It is less appropriate for 'sweet tooths', stress eaters and irregular eaters.

During stomach reduction operations, about two-thirds of the existing stomach is removed, so that the stomach reservoir is reduced in size, which again results in the patient feeling full more quickly. The removed section also contains the gland that produces the hunger-inducing hormone *ghrelin*.

Following weight loss surgery, it is better to avoid energy-rich foodstuffs that melt in the mouth and are therefore more easily absorbed. High-fat and high-fiber foods should also be avoided, because they are less easily digested.

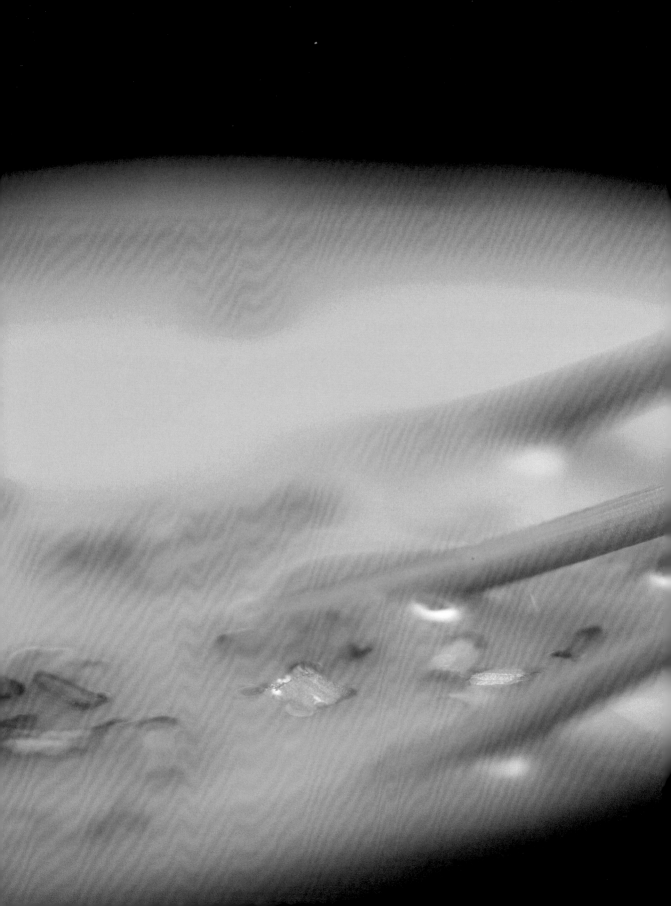

Soups

Tomato soup with mini-meatballs and basil cream

Ingredients

For the meatballs
250 g ground pork-beef
3 tablespoons
    of breadcrumbs
1 egg yolk

For the soup
500 g tomatoes
1 onion
1 liter of chicken stock
    (or two chicken stock
    cubes per liter of water)
1 tablespoon of olive oil
salt and pepper
bouquet garni
    (thyme, laurel, parsley)

For the basil cream
A handful of finely
    chopped basil
500 ml light cream
    (max. 30% fat)

Preparation

Remove the skin from the tomatoes (see the tip on the next page) and cut them into pieces.

Peel the onion and cut it into pieces. Heat the olive oil in a pan and add the onion. Cook until the onion is nicely glazed, but not brown. Add the tomatoes and cook for a few minutes more. Pour in the stock, add the bouquet garni and simmer for about 15 minutes.

In the meantime, mix together the ground meat, the breadcrumbs and the egg yolk and use this mixture to form little meatballs.

As soon as the soup has been cooked for long enough, remove the bouquet garni and blend the remaining liquid until it is smooth. Add the meatballs and allow them to cook for 10 minutes.

In the meantime, add the finely chopped basil to the cream. Season with salt and pepper. Beat the cream until it begins to stiffen.

Spoon some warm soup and a number of the meatballs into a shallow bowl and dress with the basil cream.

*Because you will find it hard to digest
unskinned tomatoes after your weight loss
operation, it is advisable to remove the skins from tomatoes.
To do this, cut a cross into the bottom of the tomato with a sharp knife
and place it in boiling water for about 10 seconds, until the corners of
the skin begin to curl. Remove from the boiling water and immerse
immediately in cold water. You will now be able to remove the skin easily.*

Roasted pumpkin soup

Ingredients

400 g pumpkin
1 skinned tomato
2 onions
1 liter of vegetable stock
1 dl light cream
    (max. 30% fat)
olive oil
2 cloves of garlic
1 tablespoon of chives
nutmeg
salt and pepper

Preparation

Pre-heat the oven to 180°C. Place the halved pumpkins (with the skin on the down side) in the oven, together with one of the onions (cut into four) and one crushed clove of garlic. Roast the pumpkin for 50 minutes, until the flesh becomes soft.

Remove the pumpkin from the oven and scoop out the flesh with a spoon. The skin of the pumpkin is not used.

Put one tablespoon of olive oil in a pan. Add the second onion, cut into pieces. Cook until the onion is nicely glazed, but not brown. Add the remaining clove of crushed garlic and cook this briefly with the onion. Finally, add the pumpkin mash and the vegetable stock.

Season according to your own preference with salt, pepper and nutmeg. Cook everything for a further 20 minutes.

Mix the soup in a blender until it has a smooth consistency.

You can make the soup more festive by adding a little light cream, some chopped chives and some slices of tomato.

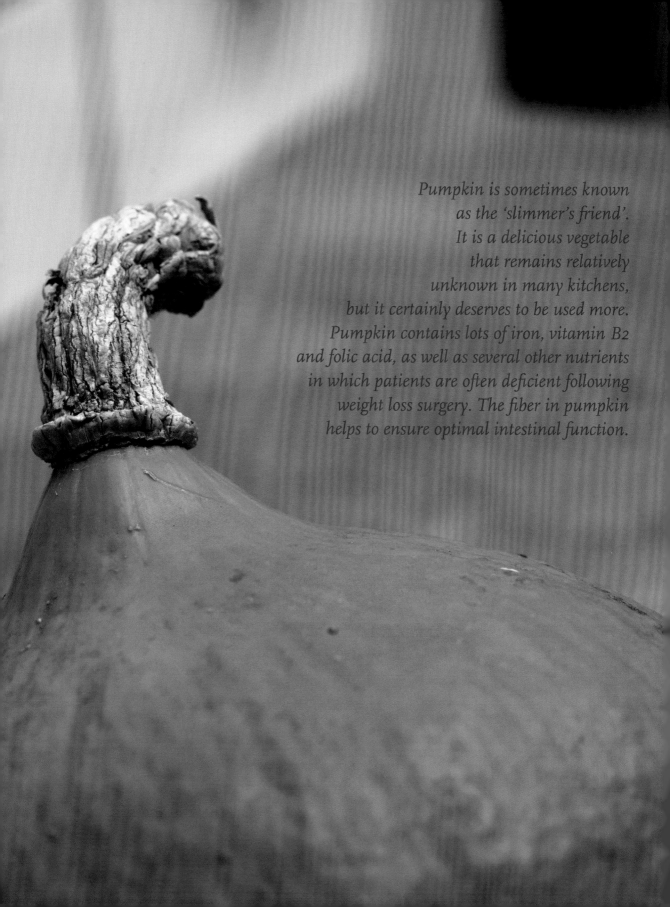

Pumpkin is sometimes known
as the 'slimmer's friend'.
It is a delicious vegetable
that remains relatively
unknown in many kitchens,
but it certainly deserves to be used more.
Pumpkin contains lots of iron, vitamin B2
and folic acid, as well as several other nutrients
in which patients are often deficient following
weight loss surgery. The fiber in pumpkin
helps to ensure optimal intestinal function.

Carrot soup
with ginger and orange

Ingredients

500 g carrots
2 onions
1 liter of chicken stock
   (or two chicken stock
   cubes per liter of water)
2 laurel leaves
2 sprigs of thyme
olive oil
salt and pepper
2 cloves of garlic
2 cm of ginger, grated
1 teaspoon of crushed
   coriander seeds
2 oranges
a few stalks of chive

Preparation

Chop the onion into fine pieces. Put a little
olive oil in a pan and cook the onion until it
is nicely glazed.

Peel the carrots and cut them into small blocks.
Add the blocks to the onion and cook them
together for a few minutes more. Stir in most
of the grated ginger.

Deglaze with the chicken stock and add the sprigs
of thyme and the laurel leaves. Bring gently to
the boil, then simmer for 20 minutes. Remove
the thyme and laurel.

Mix the soup well with a hand-mixer, pour it into
nice bowls and finish with the finely crushed
coriander seeds and the rest of the grated ginger.
Decorate with some finely chopped chives.

If the soup is too thick, you can dilute it with
the juice of two oranges. This will give the soup
a sweeter flavor.

Taste the soup and season with salt and pepper,
according to your own preference.

Carrots contain plenty of carotene,
which the body converts into
vitamin A. This vitamin is good
for your skin and your eyes.

Leek soup with Boursin (herb cheese)

Ingredients

4 leeks, finely chopped
2 onions
1 tablespoon of olive oil
1 liter of vegetable stock
4 tablespoons
    of Boursin light
salt and pepper
2 laurel leaves
2 sprigs of thyme
a few stalks of chive

Preparation

Cut the leeks into fine rings. Wash them thoroughly and let them drain. Keep a few rings to one side for the finishing.

Peel the onions and chop them into fine pieces. Put a little olive oil in a pan and cook the onion until it is nicely glazed. Add the leek rings and cook them together for a few minutes.

Pour in the vegetable stock and add salt, pepper, the sprigs of thyme and the laurel leaves. Simmer for 30 minutes. Remove the thyme and laurel.

Mix the soup well with a hand-mixer, add the remaining leek rings and cook gently for a few more minutes.

Place a tablespoon of Boursin in the middle of a shallow bowl and carefully spoon some soup around the cheese. Decorate with some finely chopped chives. Serve warm.

You can add finely
chopped shreds of
smoked salmon to give
this soup a more festive look.

You can already start eating and living more healthily before your weight loss surgery. This will make it all the easier afterwards!

Endive soup with shrimps

Ingredients

500 g endive
1 apple
1 onion
1 tablespoon of olive oil
100 g shrimps
4 tablespoons
   of low-fat yoghurt
1 lemon
2 tablespoons
   of chopped chives
1 liter of chicken stock

Preparation

Peel and chop the onion. Clean the endives and cut them into pieces. Keep some of the endive to one side for later. Peel half of the apple and cut it into small blocks.

Heat the olive oil in a pan and sauté the onion. Add the endive and the apple. Dilute with the chicken stock and simmer gently for 10 minutes with the lid on the pan, until the vegetables are nicely cooked.

Mix the soup in a blender until it has a smooth consistency.

Cut the remaining half of the apple into small blocks or rods and sprinkle them with some lemon juice, so that they do not color.
Cut the remaining endive pieces into fine strips. Stir together the shrimps, yoghurt and chives. Season with salt and pepper.

Heat the soup thoroughly. Spoon a portion of the shrimp mixture into the middle of a bowl and place some of the apple rods and the endive strips on top. Carefully add the soup around the shrimps.

Shrimps are delicious to eat and are also good for you. They contain few calories (just 1 gram of fat per 100 grams of shrimps!) and are an important source of selenium and vitamin B12. Shrimps are also easily digested by people who have undergone weight loss surgery.

Peas soup with fennel and fried bacon blocks

Ingredients

200 g smoked bacon
   blocks
1 liter of chicken stock
white part of 1 leek
500 g peas (fresh
   or deep-frozen)
1 onion
1 fennel
2 tablespoons of olive oil
2 laurel leaves
2 sprigs of thyme
salt and pepper

Preparation

Peel the onion and chop it into large pieces. Clean the white part of the leek and cut it into rings. Cut the fennel into blocks.

Heat the olive oil in a pan and sauté the onion. Add the leek and the fennel, followed by the peas. Keep 50 grams of peas to one side for the finishing.

Pour in the chicken stock and add the sprigs of thyme and the laurel leaves. Cook all the vegetables for another 20 minutes on a moderate heat, until everything is nicely cooked through. In the meantime, fry the smoked bacon blocks in some olive oil until they are crisp and golden. Turn them out onto a plate covered with a sheet of kitchen paper, so that the paper can absorb the fat.

Remove the thyme and laurel. Mix the soup to a smooth consistency. Season with salt and pepper. Remember that the bacon blocks are also salty, so you don't need to add too much!

Spoon some of the bacon blocks and the remaining peas into a bowl. Pour in some of the warm soup and serve with a warm piece of toast.

To make the soup fresher and more festive, you can add a tablespoon of Pastis (a French aperitif based on aniseed) and some fresh mint leaves.

Some patients may find the crispy bacon blocks hard
to digest at first, particularly in the period immediately
after the weight loss operation. You need to chew them
thoroughly, not just swallow them whole. If you want,
you can add the blocks to the soup after it has
been mixed and then reheat it, until
the crispy blocks become softer.
This makes them easier to eat.

Broccoli soup with ham

Ingredients

2 broccoli
2 onions
1 clove of garlic
1 liter of vegetable stock
200 g lean, smoked ham
　(in a thick slice)
1 tablespoon of olive oil
2 laurel leaves
2 sprigs of thyme
salt and pepper

Preparation

Peel the onion and chop it into large pieces. Remove the broccoli rosettes from the stem and wash them thoroughly.

Put a little olive oil in a pan and cook the onion until it is nicely glazed. Add the crushed clove of garlic and continue cooking until the aromas of the garlic are released. Add the broccoli rosettes and the vegetable stock. Keep a few of the broccoli rosettes to one side for the finishing.

Add the sprigs of thyme and the laurel leaves. Bring the mixture to the boil and simmer for 30 minutes.

In the meantime, cut the remaining broccoli rosettes into small pieces and cut the ham into small blocks.

Remove the thyme and laurel. Mix the soup with a hand-mixer until it has a smooth consistency. Season with salt and pepper.

Spoon some of the broccoli pieces and ham blocks into a bowl, before carefully adding the warm soup.

Broccoli is versatile, healthy and low in calories. This fiber-rich vegetable also helps your intestines to work properly. At the same time, broccoli is an excellent source of vitamins: a single portion of broccoli contains sufficient vitamin C to meet your daily intake requirements. Vitamin C increases bodily resistance. What's more, broccoli also contains high doses of vitamins A and K, nutrients in which patients are often deficient following weight loss surgery.

Involve your family and friends in your new lifestyle after your weight loss surgery. They will be a constant source of encouragement and support.

Zucchini-curry soup with coconut milk

Ingredients

2 zucchini
1 large onion
the white of 1 leek
1 clove of garlic
4 dl unsweetened
  coconut milk
1 liter of chicken stock
1 tablespoon of olive oil
1 tablespoon of green
  curry paste
1 clump of cilantro
salt and pepper

Preparation

Peel the onion and chop it finely. Cut the white of the leek into pieces and rinse thoroughly to remove any dirt or sand. Peel the zucchini and cut them into pieces.

Put a little olive oil in a pan and cook the onion until it is nicely glazed. Add the crushed clove of garlic and continue cooking briefly.

Add the leek, zucchini, vegetable stock and green curry paste. Season with salt and pepper. Simmer for 30 minutes on a low heat.

In the meantime, cut the stalks off the cilantro and keep the leaves for garnishing.

Mix the soup in a blender or with a hand-mixer until it is smooth and silky. Add the coconut milk. Taste the soup and add salt, pepper or curry paste, according to your personal preference.

Spoon the soup into a bowl and garnish with the cilantro leaves. This gives the soup a nice oriental touch.

NOTE:
It is not always easy to digest the skin of a zucchini after a weight loss operation. This is why the recipe says that the zucchini should be peeled. If, however, you have no trouble digesting zucchini skin, you can leave them unpeeled. The little dots of bright green add an extra color dimension to the soup.

No other vegetable can rival zucchini
when it comes to vitamin and mineral content.
They contain high amounts of potassium, magnesium,
vitamin B1, vitamin B9 and folic acid.
I cannot recommend them highly enough!

Celeriac soup with Roquefort cheese

Ingredients

1 celeriac, peeled
   and cut into blocks
the white of 1 leek,
   cut into rings
1 onion
1 clove of garlic
1 tablespoon of olive oil
1 liter of chicken stock
100 g Roquefort cheese
1 tablespoon of chives
salt and pepper

Preparation

Put a little olive oil in a pan and cook the onion until it is nicely glazed. Add the crushed clove of garlic and continue cooking until the aromas of the garlic are released. Add the celeriac and the leek and cook everything for a few more minutes. Season with salt and pepper.

Add the chicken stock to the vegetables and simmer for 30 minutes, until the celeriac is soft.

Mix the soup in a blender until it is fine and smooth. Keep the soup warm.

In the meantime, crumble the Roquefort cheese with a fork.

Spoon some soup into a bowl and add some of the Roquefort. Garnish with the chopped chives.

In addition to calcium and iron,
celeriac contains several other important vitamins:
C, B1 and B2. Tasty and healthy: what could be better!

Andalusian soup

Ingredients

1 onion
1 clove of garlic
1 stick of white celery
the white of 1 leek
1 red bell pepper
2 beef tomatoes
1 sweet red pepper
4 tablespoons
    of chopped parsley
2 tablespoons of olive oil
2 laurel leaves
2 sprigs of thyme
1 liter of vegetable stock
some garden cress
salt and pepper

Preparation

Sauté the chopped onion and the crushed garlic in a little olive oil.

Cut all the other vegetables into pieces, add them to the onion and garlic and cook for a few minutes more. Add the sprigs of thyme and laurel leaves

Pour in the vegetable stock and simmer for 30 minutes. Remove the thyme and laurel. Mix the soup with a hand-mixer until the consistency is smooth and silky. Season with salt and pepper.

Spoon some soup into a bowl and garnish with a little garden cress.

The skins of tomatoes and bell peppers are not always easily digested by people who have had weight loss surgery. Peel these vegetables before cooking or skin them after immersing them briefly in boiling water (see the recipe for tomato soup with basil cream). You can also roast bell peppers to loosen their skins.

Starters

Guacamole

Ingredients

2 avocados (ripe)
1 lime
1 clove of garlic (crushed)
1 shallot
4 tablespoons of finely
  chopped cilantro
2 tomatoes (ripe)

Preparation

Cut the avocados in two and remove the pit. Scoop out the flesh and place it in a bowl. Keep the emptied halves of skin for later.

Mash the avocado flesh with a fork, while adding the juice of half a lime, so that the flesh does not color.

Add the crushed garlic, finely chopped shallot and cilantro. Season with salt and pepper.

Peel the tomatoes, remove the seeds and cut them into pieces. Stir the tomatoes into the avocado mixture and spoon the resulting guacamole into the avocado skins: this gives the recipe a festive look!

Avocados are packed full of vitamins, such as B5, B9 (folic acid), C, E, K and B2. What's more, it also contains a number of useful minerals, like copper, potassium, iron, manganese, phosphorous and zinc. In other words, there are plenty of reasons to eat this vegetable regularly after your weight loss operation, because this type of surgery can often be followed by vitamin and mineral deficiencies.

Tuna tartare

Ingredients

200 g fresh tuna
2 tablespoons of capers
1 shallot
1 tablespoon of freshly
    chopped chives
1 lime
4 tablespoons of olive oil
1 teaspoon of wasabi
a handful of arugula
some red beet shoots
4 cherry tomatoes
salt and pepper

Preparation

Allow the tuna to stiffen in the freezer. This will make it easier to cut into neat blocks of about 0.5 centimeter.

Finely chop the shallot and the chives.

Place the tuna, shallot and chives in a bowl. Add the olive oil, capers, wasabi and the juice of a lime. Season with salt and pepper.

Stir all the ingredients carefully, so that the tuna blocks retain their shape and do not fall apart. Place the resulting mixture into the refrigerator for about 1 hour.

Fill a small bowl with the tuna tartare. Dress with arugula and beet shoots. Cut the cherry tomatoes in two and place them on top of the tartare as a garnish.

Tuna is a fish with a fibrous structure, which can be difficult to digest when cooked. Because it is important to eat fish from time to time, this tuna tartare is a useful alternative, because the blocks of fish are small. Fresh tuna is low in calories and contains plenty of calcium, iron, manganese, phosphorous, potassium and sodium, as well as several key vitamins, such as A, B1, B2, B6, C and E.

Scampi with a garlic-curry sauce and an apple salad

Ingredients

16 scampi/prawns
1 shallot
1 clove of finely
    chopped garlic
1 dl white wine
1 dl low-fat cream
curry powder
2 tablespoons of olive oil
2 tablespoons of finely
    chopped chives
1 apple (Granny Smith
    or Jonagold)
some handfuls of mache
    (corn salad)
salt and pepper

Preparation

Sauté the finely chopped onion and garlic in a little olive oil, until both are nicely glazed.

Peel the scampi and remove the intestinal tracts. Fry them briefly on a high heat in a pan with a little olive oil (no longer than two minutes, otherwise they will become rubbery).
Season with salt and pepper.

Deglaze the scampi by adding the white wine and simmer until the alcohol evaporates. Add the cream and allow the sauce to thicken. Stir in the curry powder, in a quantity that matches your personal preference.

As soon as the sauce has the required thickness, you can dress your plates. Place four scampi in the middle and pour some of the sauce over them. Garnish with a little of the finely chopped chives.

Serve with a light salad, made from a handful of mache per person, some finely chopped apple blocks and one tablespoon of olive oil. Season with salt and pepper. You don't need anything more: with scampi on your plate, you already have a festive meal!

The intestinal tract must always be removed from scampi, since they have a very bitter taste. Before cooking, cut along the back of the scampi with a sharp knife and pull out the tract, which looks like a black thread. Never cook scampi for too long; they quickly become rubbery, which makes them hard to digest.

Gazpacho with bell peppers and tomato

Ingredients

600 g fresh tomatoes
2 red bell peppers
juice of 1 lime
4 tablespoons of olive oil
2 tablespoons
  of wine vinegar
2 cloves of garlic
½ a cucumber
2 to 4 drops
  of Tabasco sauce
garden cress
salt and pepper

Preparation

Peel the tomatoes and the bell peppers. Remove the seeds and cut into small blocks.

Remove the skin from the cucumber and also cut it into small blocks.

Place all the vegetable blocks in a blender, together with the garlic, olive oil, lime juice and Tabasco. Season the resulting mixture with salt, pepper and the wine vinegar.

Allow the cold soup to stand for an hour in the refrigerator. When sufficiently cooled, pour it into some nice glass bowls and serve with a little garden cress.

This cold vegetable soup is also delicious when served warm. It is packed full of vitamins, but contains almost no calories!

Smoked trout with horseradish dressing

Ingredients

400 g smoked trout fillets
4 teaspoons of horseradish
8 tablespoons of yoghurt
2 tablespoons
   of lemon juice
2 tablespoons of sherry
1 pot of trout roe
a handful of mache
4 cherry tomatoes
salt and pepper

Preparation

Divide the trout fillets into neat and equal portions on the plates.

Mix together the yoghurt, horseradish and lemon juice. Add the sherry and season with salt and pepper.

Spoon some of the sauce over the trout and finish with some trout roe, a few mache leaves and some pieces of cherry tomato.

Delicious, quick to make and bursting with omega-3 fatty acids.

Fish is part of any healthy diet. The fatty (omega-3) acids they contain are good for the heart and arteries.

Tapenade of sun-dried tomatoes

Ingredients

200 g marinated cherry
    tomatoes
2 cloves of garlic
1 shallot
2 tablespoons of lime juice
2 tablespoons of olive oil
10 fresh basil leaves

Preparation

Tapenade is easy and quick to make and is always healthy and tasty.

Wash and drain the tomatoes. Place them in a blender with the garlic, shallot, lime juice and olive oil. Mix everything well, but not too much – you still want the tapenade to have some structure and contain some solid pieces of tomato.

Spread the tapenade on some toast and garnish with a basil leaf.

Tapenade is delicious on toasted bread, which you can cut into nice decorative triangles before serving.

Having a conscious and responsible approach to your food after your weight loss surgery will not only have an impact on your health but also on who you are as a person!

Shrimp cocktail with a dill sauce

Ingredients

150 g fresh shrimps
150 g smoked salmon
1 pot of trout roe
3 stalks of dill
1/3 of a cucumber
some cress
½ dl sour cream
½ dl light mayonnaise
1 tablespoon of whisky
1 tablespoon
    of tomato ketchup
some drops
    of Tabasco sauce
salt and pepper

Preparation

Peel the cucumber, cut it lengthways, remove the seeds and cut it into blocks of 0.5 centimeter.

Finely chop the dill, but keep a few of the feathery stems to one side for the garnishing.

Place the dill in a bowl and add the sour cream, mayonnaise, whisky and tomato ketchup. Stir well. Season with salt and pepper. You can also add some drops of Tabasco, depending on your personal preference.

Cut the smoked salmon into fine pieces.

Stir together the salmon, shrimps and cucumber blocks. Spoon portions of the resulting mixture into nice glass serving dishes.

Add a spoonful of the sauce on top and finish with the trout roe, a stem of dill and some cress.

Green tapenade with anchovies

Ingredients

250 g green olives
50 g capers
1 clove of garlic
4 tablespoons of finely
  chopped basil
4 tablespoons of olive oil
4 strips of (tinned)
  anchovy in their
  own juice
pepper

Preparation

Drain the capers and the anchovies. Mix them in a blender with the garlic and olives. Add the olive oil gradually during the blending. Do not blend for too long – you still want some structure in your tapenade. 10-15 seconds should be enough.

Season with pepper.

This tapenade is ready in seconds and is delicious served on toast, which you can cut into nice decorative shapes. Serve with some finely chopped basil.

Never use ready-made toasts from the supermarket, because these can be hard and difficult to digest after weight loss surgery. Always toast your own bread.

Mozzarella mousse with a tomato salsa

Ingredients

4 tomatoes, peeled
   and de-seeded
1 shallot
1 ball of mozzarella
   with fluid
4 tablespoons of olive oil
fresh basil
salt and pepper

Preparation

Mix the mozzarella and its fluid in a blender until it forms a mousse. Season with salt and pepper. Put the mixture into the refrigerator for 30 minutes.

In the meantime, peel and de-seed the tomatoes, before cutting them into 0.5 centimeter blocks. Finely chop the shallot.

Stir together the tomato, shallot, some finely chopped basil and some olive oil. Season with salt and pepper.

Spoon portions of the tomato salsa into nice serving dishes. Add a spoonful of the mozzarella mousse on top and garnish with a fresh basil leaf.

This starter is light, original and festive!

Main courses

Hare in a hunter's sauce with poached pear and cranberries

Ingredients

For the hare
1 hare (or 2 hare fillets
   for four people)
2 onions
4 cloves of garlic
200 g smoked bacon cubes
a slice of white bread
4 tablespoons of mustard
500 ml white wine
500 ml game stock
4 laurel leaves
4 sprigs of thyme
6 juniper berries
2 cloves
olive oil
salt and pepper

Preparation

Hare

Cut the hare into portions or ask your butcher to do it. Fry the hare in some olive oil until it is golden brown. Remove from the pan and keep to one side on a plate.

Sauté the finely chopped onion and the crushed garlic in a little olive oil. Add the bacon cubes and cook until they are also nicely browned.

Deglaze the pan by adding the white wine. Cook further until the alcohol evaporates. Add the game stock, thyme, laurel, juniper berries and cloves. Season with salt and pepper.

Place the pieces of hare into this liquid, together with a slice of white bread that has been spread with the mustard. Simmer for 2 hours, until the meat of the hare is nice and soft.

By now, the sauce will have reduced to one-third of its original volume. If this sauce is still not thick enough, you can remove the hare and reduce the sauce further. Remember to keep the hare warm.

>>

Make sure that the hare is cooked thoroughly. Meat is harder to digest if it is not soft enough.

For the poached pears
4 pears (not fully ripe)
250 ml red wine
250 ml water
1 vanilla stick
2 tablespoons of honey

For the cranberry sauce
100 g fresh cranberries
1 tablespoon of honey
a splash of water
cinnamon powder

Poached pears

Peel the pears. Pour the wine and the water into a pan. Make an incision along the length of the vanilla stick with a sharp knife and scrape out the marrow inside. Add this marrow to the water and wine. Add the honey and turn up the heat. Immerse the pears in the hot fluid and cook for 15 minutes. When the pears are just soft, remove them from the fluid, but keep them warm.

Cranberry sauce

Place the cranberries, honey and water in a pan. Bring to the boil and let the mixture simmer until the sauce reaches the right thickness. You can add cinnamon powder, depending on your personal preference.

'Bird's nests' in tomato sauce with mashed potato

Ingredients

**For the 'bird's nests'
(a kind of warm Scotch egg)**
500 g mixed ground
    pork/beef
5 eggs
4 tablespoons
    of breadcrumbs
2 tablespoons of olive oil
nutmeg
salt and pepper

For the sauce
2 onions
1 clove of garlic
1 tablespoon of olive oil
600 g tomatoes
    (de-skinned)
2 sprigs of fresh thyme
2 laurel leaves

Preparation

'Bird's nests'

Mix together the ground meat, one of the eggs and the breadcrumbs. Season with salt, pepper and nutmeg. Kneed everything well until the mixture has a firm consistency.

In the meantime, boil the remaining four eggs for 7 minutes. Remove them from the pan and place them immediately in ice-cold water, so that they can be peeled easily.

Take a quarter of the meat mixture, fold it around one of the peeled eggs and make a nice ball shape, by rolling it gently. Repeat the process for the other eggs.

Fry these four 'bird's nests' gently in olive oil, until they are golden brown. Pre-heat the oven to 180°C. Cook the 'bird's nests' in the oven for a further 10 minutes.

Sauce

Finely chop the onion and the garlic and sauté them in a little olive oil until nicely glazed.

Peel and de-seed the tomatoes, then cut them into small blocks. Add them to the onion and garlic mixture, together with a little water.   >>

For the mashed potato
1 kg potatoes
1 egg yolk
1.5 dl skimmed milk
2 tablespoons of olive oil
nutmeg
salt and pepper

Season with salt and pepper. Add the sprigs of thyme and the laurel leaves. Allow the sauce to simmer for 10 minutes. Remove the thyme and laurel. Mix the sauce finely with a hand-mixer until it has a smooth consistency.

Mashed potato

Peel the potatoes, cut them into pieces and boil them in salted water until they are cooked through.

Drain off the water and mix the cooked potatoes in a blender. Add the egg yolk, skimmed milk and olive oil. Season with salt, pepper and nutmeg. Mix thoroughly.

Cut the 'bird's nests' in half and arrange them on four warm plates. Add some of the mashed potato and tomato sauce. If desired, finish with the vegetables of your choice.

Nutritional supplements are necessary after weight loss surgery, but a varied diet also gives you plenty of vitamins.

Spicy meatballs with carrot puree

Ingredients

For the meatballs
500 g mixed ground
   pork/beef
1 onion
2 cloves of garlic,
   finely chopped
1 tablespoon
   of fresh parsley
1 tablespoon
   of fresh chives
1 tablespoon
   of paprika powder
1 teaspoon of cumin seeds
2 tablespoons of fresh
   chopped cilantro
½ teaspoon
   of cinnamon powder
4 tablespoons
   of breadcrumbs
2 eggs
4 tablespoons of olive oil

For the carrot puree
800 g potatoes
8 large carrots
1 tablespoon of olive oil
1 dl skimmed milk
nutmeg
salt and pepper

Preparation

Meatballs

Peel the onion and cut it into fine pieces.
Do the same with the garlic.

Mix together the ground meat, onion, garlic, breadcrumbs, eggs and all the herbs/spices in a large bowl. Kneed everything well until the mixture has a firm consistency. Roll the mixture into a number of small balls.

Heat the olive oil in a pan and fry the meatballs until they are golden brown and cooked through.

Carrot puree

Peel the potatoes and cut them into pieces. Peel the carrots and cut them into slices. Cook the potatoes and the carrots in a pan of boiling water with a pinch of salt until they are cooked through.

Drain off the water. Mash the cooked potatoes and carrots into a puree using a masher. Add the olive oil, salt, pepper, nutmeg and skimmed milk. Stir until smooth and creamy.

To make the puree more festive, you can add some grated ginger. This goes perfectly with the spicy meatballs.

Ground meat is something
that weight loss surgery patients
can digest without too much difficulty.
Ground veal is less fatty than ground pork,
and it is super-delicious mixed 50-50 with ground beef.

Endive puree with chicken chipolatas

Ingredients

800 g potatoes
8 large endives
4 chipolata sausages
1 onion
150 g sour cream
1 tablespoon of olive oil
salt and pepper

Preparation

Peel the potatoes, cut them into pieces and cook them in a pan of boiling water with a pinch of salt until they are cooked through. Drain off the water.

In the meantime, heat some olive oil in a pan and sauté the finely chopped onion until it is nicely glazed. Remove the outer leaves and the hard base from the endives. Also cut out the cone-shaped heart, before cutting the endives into rings.

Sauté the endives in the same pan as the onion. Add the potatoes and mash them gently with a fork. Season with salt and pepper. Add the sour cream and stir.

In the meantime, fry the chicken chipolatas until they are golden brown and cooked through.

Arrange the chipolatas on a plate and add some of the endive puree. If desired, some finely chopped raw endive can be used as a garnish.

Chipolata sausages made from chicken are much healthier
than chipolatas made from pork, because they contain much
less fat. The finely ground meat of chipolatas is more easily
digested by patients who have undergone weight loss surgery.

Endive is a nourishing vegetable with a moisture content
of more than 90%. It contains very few calories but
high levels of minerals, such as sodium, potassium,
magnesium, iron, vitamin C and vitamin B9.
Endives need to be kept in a cool, dark place.
If exposed to too much light, they quickly
become green and bitter.

Meatrolls in an onion sauce with a savoy cabbage puree

Ingredients

For the meatrolls
4 large onions
4 meatrolls (rolled fillet of
    veal, stuffed with ground
    meat, usually a mixture
    of pork and beef)
2 sprigs of thyme
4 laurel leaves
½ liter of beef stock
4 tablespoons of olive oil
nutmeg
salt and pepper

**For the savoy
cabbage puree**
½ a savoy cabbage
800 g potatoes
50 g low-fat cream
3 tablespoons of olive oil
150 g lean bacon blocks
nutmeg
salt and pepper

Preparation

Meatrolls
Peel and finely chop the onion, before sautéing it in a pan with some olive oil, until nice and brown. Add the meatrolls to the pan and cook until they are brown on all sides. Season with salt, pepper and nutmeg. Add the sprigs of thyme and the laurel leaves, before pouring in the beef stock. Allow everything to cook for another 15 minutes on a low heat with the lid on the pan. Turn the meatrolls occasionally and make sure that there is always enough liquid in the pan, so that the meat does not dry out. If necessary add some more stock or water. Keep the onion sauce for the dressing.

Savoy cabbage puree
Peel the potatoes, cut them into pieces and boil until they are cooked through. Rinse the savoy cabbage thoroughly and cut it into thin strips. Sauté the cabbage in two tablespoons of olive oil until it is just cooked. Add a splash of water. Fry the bacon blocks in a separate pan in the remaining tablespoon of olive oil. When brown, turn them out to drain on a plate covered with a sheet of kitchen paper (to absorb the fat). Mix together the cooked potatoes and the savoy cabbage. Add the low-fat cream. Season with salt, pepper and nutmeg. Stir in the fried bacon blocks. Serve one meatroll on each plate, accompanied by a portion of the savoy cabbage puree and a splash of the onion sauce.

*You can give this recipe
a more festive touch by
using brown beer instead
of beef stock.*

Veal meatloaf with ratatouille

Ingredients

For the veal meatloaf
800 g ground veal
1 egg
4 tablespoons
   of breadcrumbs
1 onion, finely chopped
1 clove of garlic,
   finely chopped
2 tablespoons of chives
2 tablespoons of parsley
2 tablespoons of olive oil
nutmeg
salt and pepper

For the ratatouille
2 onions, finely chopped
2 red bell peppers,
   de-skinned
2 zucchini, de-skinned
1 eggplant
4 tomatoes, de-skinned
2 cloves of garlic, crushed
4 tablespoons of olive oil
salt and pepper

Preparation

Veal meatloaf

Mix all the ingredients together in a bowl. Season with salt, pepper and nutmeg.

Pre-heat the oven to 180°C. Roll the mixture into a nice ball and place it in an oven dish.

Put the dish in the oven and allow the meatloaf to cook for 30 to 40 minutes, while you prepare the ratatouille.

When ready, remove the meatloaf from the oven and let it rest for 5 minutes under a sheet of aluminum kitchen foil.

Ratatouille

Peel and finely chop the onion. Sauté it in a pan with some olive oil, until nicely glazed. Crush the garlic in a garlic press and add it to the pan.

Peel the red bell peppers and cut them into blocks of roughly 0.5 centimeter. Peel the zucchini, cut them lengthways, remove the seeds and cut them into blocks of roughly 0.5 centimeter. Also cut the eggplant into blocks of the same size.

Add all the vegetable blocks to the pan with the onion and garlic, and cook for about 5 minutes.

>>

In the meantime, peel and de-seed the tomatoes, before cutting them into blocks of 1 centimeter. Add them to the other vegetables. Put a lid on the pan and simmer all the ingredients for another 20 minutes.

When the sauce is ready, cut the meatloaf into slices. Arrange the slices on the serving plates and add some of the ratatouille alongside.

This dish is full of vitamins, thanks to the large number of vegetables it uses. You can serve it with mashed potatoes, if you wish, but this is not really necessary. This is good enough to eat without potatoes. Boiled rice is also an alternative.
Make sure you don't cook the meatloaf for too long; otherwise it will dry out and become more difficult to digest for people who have had weight loss surgery.

Italian-style stuffed pork tenderloin with salad

Ingredients

For the pork tenderloin
2 pork tenderloins
1 ball of mozzarella
8 sun-dried tomatoes
8 fresh basil leaves
8 olives, cut into slices
4 tablespoons
    of breadcrumbs
olive oil
salt and pepper
kitchen string
    or cocktail sticks

For the salad (per person)
1 handful of mixed salad
3 cherry tomatoes
1 tablespoon of
    Italian herbs
1 tablespoon of olive oil
salt and pepper

Preparation

Make a lengthways incision in the pork tenderloins, leaving the last centimeter of meat uncut. Season with salt and pepper. Cut the mozzarella into slices and place these into the opening you have made in the tenderloins. Do the same with slices of sun-dried tomatoes, the finely chopped fresh basil and the slices of olive.

Fold the tenderloins back into their original roll shape. Make sure that they remain closed during cooking by tying them with kitchen string or skewering them with cocktail sticks. Fry the tenderloins in some olive oil until they are brown on all sides. Add a splash of water to the pan, cover with a lid and allow to cook for a further 15 to 20 minutes, occasionally turning the tenderloins. If necessary, add more water. It is important that the cooking juices do not reduce completely; otherwise the meat will stick to the pan and burn.

In the meantime, prepare the salad by stirring together the mixed salad and the halved cherry tomatoes in a large bowl. Stir up the olive oil with the Italian herbs and add it to the salad. Season with salt and pepper. When the tenderloins are cooked, remove the kitchen string (or cocktail sticks). Cut the pork into generous slices and arrange them on the serving plates. Serve with the bowl of salad.

There are countless ways you can vary the use of salad. In this recipe it is your source of vitamins. Do not let the meat dry out during cooking; otherwise you will find it more difficult to eat. Dry meat can sometimes stay lodged in your digestive system. Cut your meat into small pieces and chew it well before swallowing.

Fried plaice with a roasted pumpkin puree

Ingredients

4 fillets of plaice
   (120-150 g per person)
4 tablespoons of olive oil
2 tablespoons of flour
400 g potatoes
400 g pumpkin
2 onions
1 clove of garlic, crushed
1 dl skimmed milk
1 tablespoon of olive oil
1 tablespoon
   of chopped chives
nutmeg
salt and pepper

Preparation

Pre-heat the oven to 180°C. Place the halved pumpkins (with the skin on the down side) in the oven, together with one of the onions (cut into four) and the crushed clove of garlic. Roast the pumpkin for 50 minutes, until the flesh becomes soft.

Remove the pumpkin from the oven and scoop out the flesh with a spoon. The skin of the pumpkin is not used.

Peel the potatoes, cut them into equal pieces and cook them in a pan of boiling water with a pinch of salt until they are cooked through. When ready, drain off the water.

Place the roasted pumpkin flesh and the boiled potatoes in a blender. Add the skimmed milk, olive oil, nutmeg, salt and pepper. Mix thoroughly until the puree is nice and smooth.

In the meantime, fry the plaice fillets. First rinse and dry them, then sprinkle them with a little flour. Heat some olive oil in a pan and cook the fish on a medium heat for a maximum of five minutes on each side, until they are golden brown.

Arrange the plaice on the serving plates, add some of the pumpkin puree and garnish both elements with a sprinkling of chopped chives.

Plaice is a very lean species of fish (just 1-2% fat).
Fish in general is an excellent source of protein and vitamin D.
Fish also contains several important minerals,
such as potassium, selenium and iodine.
Omega-3 is a specific fatty acid that helps
to reduce the risk of heart and vascular disease
and is present in high quantities in fish.

Avoid high-fat, sugar-rich snacks and drinks. In fact, try to avoid high-calorie foods in general.

Poached salmon with a spinach puree

Ingredients

4 fillets of fresh salmon
  (120-150 g per person)
4 tablespoons
  of lemon juice
6 tablespoons of olive oil
400 ml fish stock
800 g potatoes
400 g young spinach
2 dl skimmed milk
1 egg yolk
2 tablespoons
  of chopped chives
nutmeg
salt and pepper

Preparation

Peel the potatoes and cut them into equal pieces. Bring some water with a little salt to the boil. Add the potatoes and cook them until they are cooked through.

In the meantime, wash and drain the spinach leaves. Put two tablespoons of olive oil in a pan and sauté the spinach for a couple of minutes. Keep a few of the leaves to one side to use as a garnish. The spinach will reduce considerably volume while in the pan.

When the potatoes are ready, drain off the water. Add the spinach, two tablespoons of olive oil, the egg yolk, nutmeg, salt and pepper. Mash all the ingredients together with a masher.

Place the salmon fillets in a deep pan. Pour two tablespoons of olive oil and four tablespoons of lemon juice over the fillets. Season with salt and pepper. Add enough fish stock, so that the fillets are just covered. Place the pan in a microwave or steamer, until the fish is cooked through. Alternatively, you can poach the fish in the pan on a low heat, until it is soft and pink inside.

Arrange the fillets with some of the spinach puree and the chopped chives on the serving plates. Add some of the whole spinach leaves as a garnish.

Spinach is one of the healthiest of all vegetables and is bursting with vitamins K, A, B2, C, B6 and folic acid. It also contains magnesium, iron, calcium, potassium, copper, zinc and selenium.

Always use young spinach! Older spinach has thicker veins that are much harder to digest for people who have had weight loss surgery. If you find that you also have trouble digesting the fibers in young spinach, you can mix the puree in a blender instead of mashing it with a hand masher.

Quiche with leek and ham

Ingredients

2 leeks, cut into fine rings
250 g lean ham blocks
2 tablespoons of olive oil
4 eggs
1 dl skimmed milk
100 g low-fat Emmental
    or Gruyere cheese,
    grated
salt and pepper

Preparation

Fry the ham blocks in a pan with one tablespoon of olive oil.

Beat together the eggs and milk in a bowl. Season with salt and pepper. Add the grated cheese and stir well.

Sauté the leek in a pan until it is almost (but not quite) cooked through.

Pour the egg mixture and one tablespoon of olive oil into a greased baking dish. Spread the leek and the ham blocks evenly throughout the mixture.

Place the quiche in an oven pre-heated to 180°C and cook for 30 minutes.

Cut the quiche into triangular slices and serve with a salad.

This quiche is made without pastry, which not only helps to reduce the fat content in the recipe, but also makes it easier for weight loss patients to eat, because there are no hard, crusty pieces that may 'lodge' in the digestive system.

Quiche with scampi and broccoli

Ingredients

1 sheet of puff pastry
1 broccoli
4 eggs
1 dl skimmed milk
8 scampi
100 g low-fat Emmental
   or Gruyere cheese,
   grated
salt and pepper

Preparation

Line a baking dish with the sheet of puff pastry. Press the pastry firmly into place and prick the bottom two or three times with a fork.

Wash the broccoli and remove the rosettes. Boil the broccoli in salted water until almost (but not quite) cooked through. When ready, drain the broccoli through a strainer.

In the meantime, beat together the eggs and milk in a bowl. Season with salt and pepper. Add the grated cheese and stir well.

Peel and fry the scampi (having first removed the intestinal tracts) in a little olive oil.

Pour the egg mixture into the pastry base. Spread the scampi and broccoli rosettes evenly throughout the mixture.

Place the quiche in an oven pre-heated to 180°C and cook for 30 minutes.

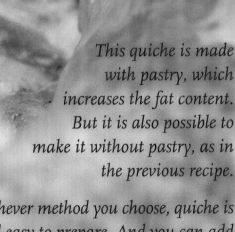

This quiche is made with pastry, which increases the fat content. But it is also possible to make it without pastry, as in the previous recipe.

Whichever method you choose, quiche is quick and easy to prepare. And you can add almost any vegetables you like! Some good combinations are endive and ham, zucchini and bacon, salmon and dill, pumpkin, spinach and shrimps.

Leek puree with mackerel sautéed in its skin

Ingredients

500 g potatoes
1 bundle of leeks
   (white part only)
nutmeg
salt and pepper
5 tablespoons of olive oil
1 dl skimmed milk
8 mackerel fillets
   (cleaned but
   not skinned)
4 tablespoons of flour

Preparation

Leek puree

Peel the potatoes and cut them into pieces. Cut the leek whites into fine rings and rinse thoroughly, to remove any sand or dirt. Cook the potatoes and the leek in a pan of boiling water with a pinch of salt. When the vegetables are cooked through, drain off the water and mash them with a masher. Add one tablespoon of olive oil, the skimmed milk, nutmeg, salt and pepper. Stir well until the puree is smooth and creamy.

Sautéed mackerel

Rinse the mackerel fillets. Pat them dry with some kitchen paper and sprinkle one tablespoon of flour on each fish (two fillets). Sauté the fillets in four tablespoons of olive oil until they are golden brown. Cover the pan with a lid and allow the fish to cook through for a further five minutes.

Mackerel is a fish that can be cooked and eaten whole, but you can also have it filleted, as in this recipe, so that you don't need to remove the bones yourself. Don't eat the mackerel skin, since this is difficult for weight loss patients to digest.

Other than that, mackerel is an excellent fish that is good for both body and mind. It is perfect as part of a healthy diet and is packed with omega-3 fatty acids, which help to prevent heart and vascular disease. What's more, it is also an important source of minerals (calcium, phosphorous, magnesium) and vitamins (A, D, B12 and K).

Cod with sautéed mushrooms

Ingredients

4 fillets of cod
4 tablespoons of olive oil
250 g mushrooms
salt and pepper

Preparation

Rinse the fish and pat it dry with some kitchen paper.

Heat the pan at high temperature and add two tablespoons of olive oil. Place the cod fillets in the pan, skin side down. Reduce the heat and cook the cod for 5 minutes. Turn the fillets and cook them on the other side, also for 5 minutes. Thicker fillets may take a little longer to cook. Season with salt and pepper.

In the meantime, warm two tablespoons of olive oil in a second pan. Brush the mushrooms clean, so that all sand or dirt is removed. Sauté the mushrooms in the pan, until they are golden brown. Season with salt and pepper according to your personal preference.

Serve the fish and the mushrooms together on a pre-warmed plate.

You can either cook the mushrooms whole (in which case you should choose smaller ones) or in slices (in which case you can use bigger ones).

Stuffed eggplant with spicy ground lamb and a tomato coulis

Ingredients

For the tomato coulis
2 eggplants
4 tomatoes
1 large onion,
   finely chopped
1 clove of garlic
4 tablespoons of olive oil
4 laurel leaves
2 sprigs of thyme
1 tablespoon of cilantro,
   finely chopped
salt and pepper

For the stuffed eggplants
400 g ground lamb
1 onion, finely chopped
1 clove of garlic,
   finely chopped
1 egg yolk
4 tablespoons
   of breadcrumbs
salt and pepper

Preparation

Peel the tomatoes, remove the seeds and cut them into small blocks. Peel and finely chop the onion and the garlic. Cut the eggplants in two. Remove the flesh and cut it into chunks. Keep the empty skins to one side for later.

Cook the finely chopped onion and garlic in the olive oil, until they are nicely glazed. Add the other vegetables and season with salt and pepper. Add the laurel leaves and the sprigs of thyme. Place a lid on the pan and simmer for 20 minutes. Remove the laurel and thyme. If you want a proper coulis, this sauce must now be mixed thoroughly with a hand-mixer. If you prefer a sauce with more structure and solid pieces of vegetable, leave the sauce as it is.

Mix together the ground lamb, breadcrumbs and egg yolk. Add the finely chopped onion and garlic. Season with salt and pepper. Stir thoroughly. Use this mixture to fill up the empty eggplant skins. Cook the stuffed eggplants for 40 minutes in a pre-heated oven at 180°C. Remove the eggplants from the oven, arrange them on serving plates and spoon over some of the tomato coulis. Garnish with the finely chopped cilantro. This dish is delicious with boiled rice.

Hamburger with sautéed leek and a garlic puree

Ingredients

4 hamburgers
1 bundle of leeks
  (white part only)
6 tablespoons of olive oil

For the garlic puree
800 g potatoes
4 cloves of garlic
1 egg yolk
1 dl skimmed milk
nutmeg
salt and pepper

Preparation

Peel the potatoes, cut them into pieces and cook them in boiling water with a little salt.

In the meantime, peel the garlic, chop it finely and sauté it in two tablespoons of olive oil, until its aromas are released.

Rinse the leek and cut it into fine rings. Sauté the rings for 20 minutes in two tablespoons of olive oil. Add a little water, if necessary, so that the leek does not stick to the pan and burn.

When the potatoes are cooked through, drain off the water from the pan. Add the sautéed garlic, egg yolk, nutmeg, salt and pepper. Mash with a masher, until the puree is smooth and creamy.

In the meantime, fry the hamburgers on both sides in two tablespoons of olive oil, until they are cooked through.

Arrange the hamburgers on serving plates and add portions of sautéed leek and garlic puree.

Desserts

Crème brûlée

Ingredients

150 g cream (30% fat)
2 dl skimmed milk
1 teaspoon of sweetener
1 vanilla stick
6 egg yolks
4 teaspoons of fine sugar

Preparation

Beat together the egg yolks and the sweetener in a bowl until they form a smooth and silky mixture. Add the cream and the milk.

Make an incision along the length of the vanilla stick with a sharp knife and scrape out the marrow inside. Add this marrow to the mixture and beat well.

Pour the mixture into a number of heat-resistant dishes and cook for 15 to 20 minutes in a pre-heated oven at 180°C.

When ready, remove the crème brûlées from the oven and allow them to cool down. When sufficiently cooled, place them in the refrigerator.

Just before serving, sprinkle the top of each crème brûlée with a teaspoon of fine sugar. Burn this sugar brown, using a kitchen blow-torch. If you do not have a blow-torch, place them under a grill at high temperature until the sugar turns golden brown (but not too dark!).

Banana milkshake

Ingredients

1 liter of skimmed milk
1 small bag of vanilla sugar
4 bananas
4 scoops of low-fat
   ice-cream

Preparation

Cut the bananas into equal pieces and mix them in a blender with the milk, ice-cream and sugar, until the mixture is smooth and lump-free.

Serve in nice glasses.

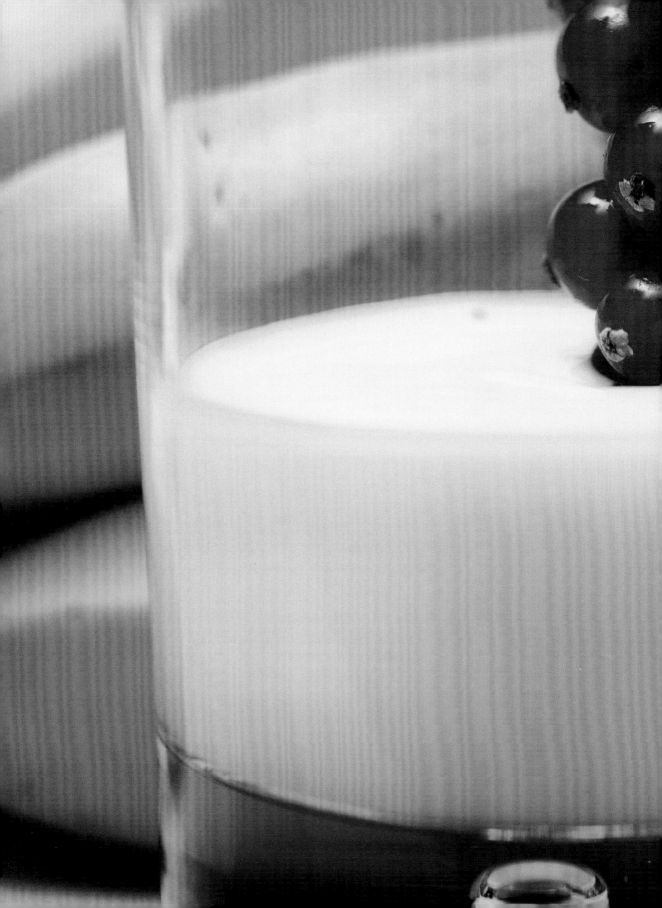

Sabayon with blackberries

Ingredients

4 eggs
1 tablespoon
    of liquid sweetener
some white wine
    (preferably sweet)
blackberries

Preparation

Separate the eggs and put the yolks into a pan. The egg whites are not needed for this recipe. Keep one of the egg shell halves to use as a measure. Add one tablespoon of liquid sweetener and eight egg shells of white wine to the egg yolks.

Place the pan with the mixture on a low heat and continue stirring/whisking all the time. Make sure you keep the temperature low; if it is too high, the eggs will start to congeal, so that you will have an omelet instead of a sabayon!

Keep stirring/whisking until the sabayon becomes thicker and frothier. Remove the pan from the heat, but continue stirring until the sabayon cools down a little. You can do this with a hand-mixer instead of a whisk, but make sure you use the whisking attachments and not the mixing ones!

Pour the sabayon into glass dishes and add a blackberry or two on top. You can also serve the dishes on a plate, so that you can add extra blackberries. Serve promptly, otherwise the blackberries will sink into the sabayon and the nice visual effect will be lost.

Cottage cheese with crumble and a raspberry coulis

Ingredients

500 g low-fat
    cottage cheese
4 tablespoons of honey
8 tablespoons
    of breakfast cereal
a handful of walnuts
250 g raspberries
the juice of 1 lemon
1 teaspoon of sweetener

Preparation

First make the raspberry coulis, but keep a number of raspberries to one side for later.

Put all the remaining raspberries in a blender and mix them to a fine consistency. If you have trouble digesting the seeds, you can pass the resulting mixture through a fine sieve.

Simmer the raspberry mix on a low heat in a pan, together with the sweetener and the lemon juice. Allow the mixture to reduce until the coulis has reached the right thickness.

Put a spoonful of honey into the bottom of each serving dish. Fill the dishes up to half way with cottage cheese. Add a layer of crushed breakfast cereal (corn flakes, etc.), followed by another layer of cottage cheese.

Finish by adding two tablespoons of the raspberry coulis to each dish, topped with some whole raspberries, some more of the crushed cereal and some chopped walnuts as decoration.

There is no need to add sugar to the cottage cheese, because you have already used honey and there will also be a hint of sweetness in the breakfast cereal, the walnuts and the raspberry coulis. A delicious dessert – and completely sugar-free!

You can add some chopped walnuts to the breakfast cereal layer. Walnuts are full of valuable nutrients (omega-3 fatty acids, fibers, proteins, vitamins and minerals) and healthy fats. They also lower levels of cholesterol in the blood.
Don't add the nut/cereal layer in the weeks immediately following your weight loss operation, since you may find them hard to digest at this early stage. But you can still make the recipe using just the cottage cheese and the raspberry coulis.

Smoothie with kiwi, banana and orange juice

Ingredients

4 kiwi fruits
4 bananas
2 dl orange juice (fresh)

Preparation

Peel the kiwis and cut them in two. Remove any hard parts and cut the remaining fruit into smaller pieces.

Peel the bananas and cut them into pieces.

Put all the fruit into a blender with the orange juice and mix until smooth and silky.

Pour the smoothie carefully into a glass and wedge a piece of kiwi onto the edge of the glass as decoration.

Fruit smoothies are a great source of vitamins. They are also ideal for the first (liquid) phase after your weight loss operation.

Smoothie with raspberry, banana and yoghurt

Ingredients

250 g raspberries
1 banana
8 tablespoons
  of low-fat yoghurt
4 teaspoons of honey

Preparation

Peel the banana and cut it into pieces.

Keep a number of raspberries to one side for later.
Put all the remaining raspberries in a blender
with the banana pieces and the yoghurt. Mix until
smooth and silky.

Put a teaspoon of honey in the bottom of
each serving glass, before carefully adding the
smoothie. Decorate with one or two of the whole
raspberries that you saved earlier.

You can also use deep-freeze raspberries. These will make your smoothie ice-cold. The banana and the honey add some sweetness to the recipe, so that you do not need to use any extra sugar.

Smoothie with banana, apple and orange juice

Ingredients

2 bananas
2 apples (sweet)
2 dl orange juice (fresh)

Preparation

Peel the bananas and cut them into equal pieces.

Peel the apples, remove the cores and cut them into blocks.

Put the banana, apple and orange juice into a blender. Mix until smooth and silky.

Pour the smoothie into glass dishes and serve immediately.

If you find the consistency of the smoothie too thick, you can dilute the mixture with 2 dl of skimmed milk. This will turn your smoothie into a real vitamin bomb, with added calcium. Quick, delicious and healthy!

Smoothie with blueberries

Ingredients

200 g blueberries
400 g low-fat yoghurt
2 dl orange juice (fresh)

Preparation

Keep a number of blueberries to one side for later.

Put all the remaining blueberries into a blender with the yoghurt and the orange juice.
Mix until smooth and silky.

Pour the smoothie into serving glasses and decorate with one or two of the whole blueberries you saved earlier.

You can freeze in blueberries, so that they make your smoothie nice and cold when you use them. This smoothie is delicious as an afternoon snack and is packed with vitamins and health-giving milk products.

Smoothie with red currants and banana

Ingredients

200 g red currants
1 banana
2 dl orange juice (fresh)

Preparation

Rinse the red currents and remove them from their stems. Keep a few of the currants to one side for later.

Peel the banana and cut it into pieces.

Put the currants, banana and orange juice into a blender. Mix until smooth and silky.

Pour the smoothie into glass dishes and decorate with some of the red currants you saved earlier.

Currants – both red and white – are good for you.
If you find them slightly too sour, you can add a teaspoon
of honey to the bottom of each serving dish before
pouring in the smoothie. This particular
smoothie has a wonderful color, so that
the kids will love eating it as well.

Chocolate mousse

Ingredients

5 egg whites
5 teaspoons of sweetener
5 pieces of chocolate
some white chocolate
   (optional)

Preparation

Melt the chocolate in a pan over a low heat, so that the chocolate does not burn.

Beat the egg whites in a bowl until they become stiff. Add the sweetener a spoonful at a time and continue beating.

Using a spatula, fold the melted chocolate carefully into the egg white mixture, so that the mousse remains light and fluffy.

If desired, you can decorate the mousse with flakes of white chocolate.

This chocolate mousse is much lower
in calories than a 'classic' mousse with
cream, sugar and egg yolks, but it is
a tasty alternative for patients who
need to avoid 'calorie bombs'
after their weight loss surgery.

"I enjoy having a beautifully dressed plate of food at a beautifully decorated table, surrounded by all my family and friends. All these things must still be possible after weight loss surgery."

Epilogue

We all want to be healthy and we all want to go through life with a body that radiates vitality and energy. But life does not always turn out the way we would like. It is so easy to say: 'Eat less, exercise more'. But it is often so difficult to do. A whole range of factors, including medical conditions, mean  that losing weight is sometimes much harder than we think. It is a great relief in these circumstances if you can ask for advice from a doctor who will listen to you and is ready to help with expert guidance. Expert but also engaged. In short, a doctor who is genuinely concerned about your welfare and who wants you to start living a healthier life even before your operation – and certainly after it. Professor Kristel De Vogelaere is this kind of doctor. I first got to know her during a postgraduate training session at the Free University of Brussels. It was fantastic to see how we were immediately on the same wavelength; how she also argued passionately that living your life in accordance with healthy principles is the only way to achieve lasting health benefits. She inspires her patients by motivating them not only to eat responsibly, but also to take exercise each day and to mentally 'retrain' themselves to think more positively and more healthily.

I have been impressed by the way Professor De Vogelaere makes her patients aware that a weight loss operation is not a final destination, but is simply a starting point for a new and healthier life journey. It touches me to see how she regards her patients not as hopeless cases, lacking in character, but as people who are still in control of their destiny and have therefore had the courage to seek help. Because it does require courage to ask for this kind of drastic help, when you are unable to control the behavior of your own body, with life-threatening conditions as a consequence. But it strengthens your courage and your resolve when you are treated by a doctor who is also concerned about your welfare after the weight loss operation.

This is exceptional by any standards. But it is even more exceptional when a doctor takes the time to write an accessible and inspirational cookbook as an additional aid for her patients. This says much about Kristel de Vogelaere both as a doctor and as a human being. She does not look on people simply as 'patients' with a complaint. Instead, she sees the whole person, the person behind the complaint, and she treats them accordingly. This is a rare gift. Almost everyone who suffers from obesity also suffers from low self-esteem, low self-respect and has no real sense of their own value. The feeling that these people get when the doctor who operated on them also stands alongside them in the kitchen is indescribable. It is the best possible encouragement to keep them on the healthy and energetic path on which they have embarked.

Sonja Kimpen

Master of Movement Sciences,
author and health coach

Index

of main ingredients

Used measures

WEIGHTS FOR DRY INGREDIENTS

50g	2oz
75g	3oz
100g	3½oz
125g	4oz
150g	5oz
175g	6oz
200g	7oz
250g	9oz
300g	11oz
350g	12oz
400g	14oz
450g	1lb
500g	1lb 2oz
600g	1lb 5oz

LIQUID MEASURES

50ml	2fl oz	¼ cup
100ml	3½fl oz	
150ml	5fl oz	
175ml	6fl oz	¾ cup
200ml	7fl oz	
250ml	8fl oz	1 cup
500 ml	16 fl oz	2 cups/1 pint
1 litre	1¾ pints	1 quart

OVEN TEMPERATURES

°C	°F
160	325
180	350

www.lannoo.com

Register on our web site and we will regularly send you a newsletter
with information about new books and interesting, exclusive offers.

Text: Professor Kristel De Vogelaere
Photography: Thierry Van Vreckem
Layout: Michel Van Wambeke
Translation: Ian Connerty
Original edition: 2014 by De Draak vzw, Tollembeek

If you have remarks or questions, please contact our editors:
redactielifestyle@lannoo.com

© Lannoo Publishers, Tielt, 2015
D/2015/45/286 - NUR 440-443
ISBN 978 94 014 2813 2